MAY THE LORD BLESS YOU!

"May God be merciful to you, bless you, and cause his face to shine on you. Selah." Psalm 67:1 (WEB)

"God, you are my God.
    I will earnestly seek you.
My soul thirsts for you.
    My flesh longs for you,
    in a dry and weary land,
where there is no water.
2 So I have seen you in the sanctuary,
    watching your power and your glory.
3 Because your loving kindness is better than life,
    my lips shall praise you.
4 So I will bless you while I live.
    I will lift up my hands in your name.
5 My soul shall be satisfied as with the richest food.
    My mouth shall praise you with joyful lips,
6   when I remember you on my bed,
    and think about you in the night watches.
7 For you have been my help.
    I will rejoice in the shadow of your wings.
8 My soul stays close to you.
    Your right hand holds me up."

"DON'T LET YOUR HEART BE TROUBLED. BELIEVE IN GOD. BELIEVE ALSO IN ME.

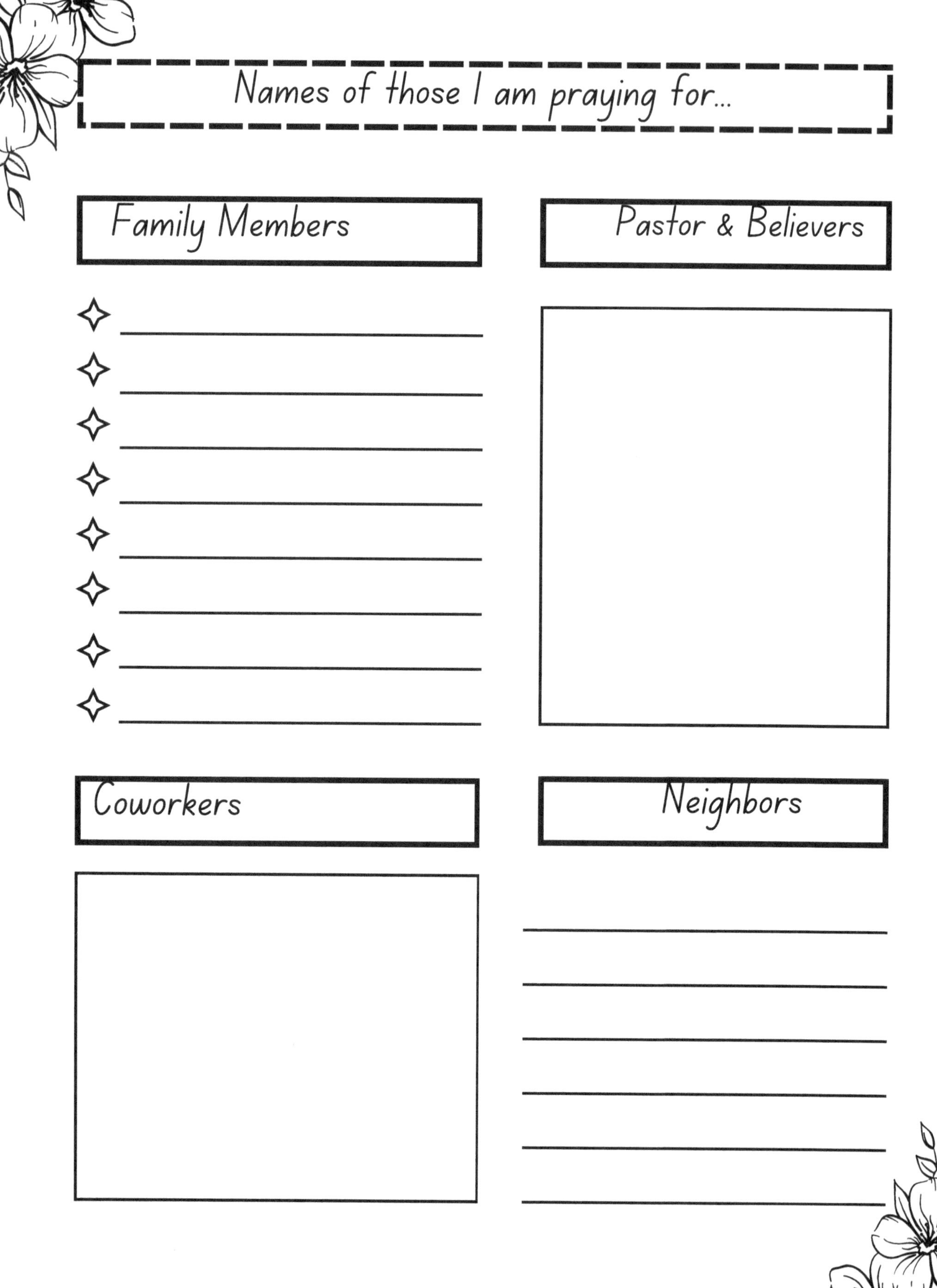

Names of those I am praying for...
Family Members
Pastor & Believers
Coworkers
Neighbors

Dear Heavenly Father,

Date: ______________

____

____

____

____

____

____

____

____

____

____

____

____

____

Hope is Alive

Hope is Alive

Dear Heavenly Father,

Date:

Hope is Alive

Dear Heavenly Father,

Date:

Hope is Alive

Hope is Alive

Dear Heavenly Father,   Date:

Hope is Alive

Hope is Alive

Dear Heavenly Father,   Date:

Hope is Alive

Hope is Alive

Dear Heavenly Father,   Date:

____

____

____

____

____

____

____

____

____

____

____

____

____

____

Hope is Alive

Hope is Alive

Dear Heavenly Father,   Date:

Hope is Alive

Hope is Alive

Dear Heavenly Father,

Date:

Hope is Alive

Hope is Alive

Hope is Alive

Dear Heavenly Father,   Date:

Hope is Alive

Hope is Alive

Dear Heavenly Father,   Date:

____

____

____

____

____

____

____

____

____

____

____

____

____

____

____

Hope is Alive

Hope is Alive

Dear Heavenly Father,

Date:

Hope is Alive

Hope is Alive

Dear Heavenly Father,

Date:

____

____

____

____

____

____

____

____

____

____

____

____

____

____

____

____

Hope is Alive

Hope is Alive

Dear Heavenly Father,   Date:

Hope is Alive

Hope is Alive

Dear Heavenly Father,

Date:

Hope is Alive

Hope is Alive

Dear Heavenly Father,

Date:

Hope is Alive

Hope is Alive

Dear Heavenly Father,   Date:

____

____

____

____

____

____

____

____

____

____

____

____

____

____

____

____

Hope is Alive

Hope is Alive

Dear Heavenly Father,   Date:

Hope is Alive

Hope is Alive

Dear Heavenly Father,   Date:

Hope is Alive

Quotes, Notes, and Drawings

Hope is Alive

Dear Heavenly Father,   Date:

Hope is Alive

Hope is Alive

Dear Heavenly Father,   Date:

Hope is Alive

Hope is Alive

Dear Heavenly Father,   Date:

Hope is Alive

Hope is Alive

Dear Heavenly Father,   Date:

Hope is Alive

Hope is Alive

Dear Heavenly Father,   Date:

Hope is Alive

Hope is Alive

Dear Heavenly Father,   Date:

Hope is Alive

Hope is Alive

Dear Heavenly Father,   Date:

____

____

____

____

____

____

____

____

____

____

____

____

____

____

Hope is Alive

Hope is Alive

Dear Heavenly Father,

Date:

Hope is Alive

Hope is Alive

Dear Heavenly Father,

Date:

Hope is Alive

Hope is Alive

Dear Heavenly Father,   Date:

____

____

____

____

____

____

____

____

____

____

____

____

____

____

____

Hope is Alive

Hope is Alive

Dear Heavenly Father,   Date:

____

____

____

____

____

____

____

____

____

____

____

____

____

____

Hope is Alive

Hope is Alive

Dear Heavenly Father,

Date:

Hope is Alive

Hope is Alive

Dear Heavenly Father,

Date:

Hope is Alive

Hope is Alive

Dear Heavenly Father,   Date:

____

____

____

____

____

____

____

____

____

____

____

____

____

____

____

____

Hope is Alive

Dear Heavenly Father,

Date:

Hope is Alive

Hope is Alive

Dear Heavenly Father,   Date:

Hope is Alive

Hope is Alive

Dear Heavenly Father,   Date:

Hope is Alive

Hope is Alive

Dear Heavenly Father,   Date:

Hope is Alive

Hope is Alive

Dear Heavenly Father,

Date:

Hope is Alive

Hope is Alive

Dear Heavenly Father,   Date:

____

____

____

____

____

____

____

____

____

____

____

____

____

____

Hope is Alive

Hope is Alive

Dear Heavenly Father,   Date:

Hope is Alive

Hope is Alive

Dear Heavenly Father,   Date:

____

____

____

____

____

____

____

____

____

____

____

____

____

Hope is Alive

Hope is Alive

Dear Heavenly Father,

Date:

Hope is Alive

Hope is Alive

Dear Heavenly Father,   Date:

Hope is Alive

Hope is Alive

Dear Heavenly Father,

Date:

Hope is Alive

Hope is Alive

Dear Heavenly Father,

Date:

____

Hope is Alive

Dear Heavenly Father,   Date:

____

____

____

____

____

____

____

____

____

____

____

____

____

____

____

Hope is Alive

Hope is Alive

Dear Heavenly Father,   Date:

Hope is Alive

Hope is Alive

Dear Heavenly Father,   Date:

Hope is Alive

Hope is Alive

Dear Heavenly Father,   Date:

____

____

____

____

____

____

____

____

____

____

____

____

____

____

____

Hope is Alive

Hope is Alive

Dear Heavenly Father,   Date:

Hope is Alive

Hope is Alive

Dear Heavenly Father,   Date:

Hope is Alive

Hope is Alive

Dear Heavenly Father,   Date:

Hope is Alive

Hope is Alive

Dear Heavenly Father,   Date:

Hope is Alive

Hope is Alive

Dear Heavenly Father,   Date:

____

____

____

____

____

____

____

____

____

____

____

____

____

____

____

____

Hope is Alive

Hope is Alive

Dear Heavenly Father,   Date:

____

____

____

____

____

____

____

____

____

____

____

____

____

____

____

____

Hope is Alive

Hope is Alive

Dear Heavenly Father,   Date:

Hope is Alive

Hope is Alive

Dear Heavenly Father,   Date:

Hope is Alive

Hope is Alive

Hope is Alive